God's Love is Real

Maria Elena Garza

To order additional copies of this book, contact:
Xlibris
1-888-795-4274
www.Xlibris.com
Orders@Xlibris.com

Angel in Spring

An angel came the other day
It was a sunny day in May
She just came by
And
Picked a flower
She looked at it and smiled
She put it down again
Walked away into the day
And then she turned and looked
At me
And all she did was
Smile...

An Angel Sat atop a Hill

An angel sat
Atop a hill
Amongst the soft green grass

The gentle wind
Brushed its wings
And the evening sun just watched

High above
The angel sat and smiled

Below the hill
The town was still
The wind was calm
The day had gone

The stars
Twinkled
Danced
And watched
The angel

He just sat atop a hill
And smiled

Resting Angel

I thought I saw an angel
One day…
Not long ago

Everything was still
No one was around

I thought I saw an angel
He came and stayed a while
He never said one word
He just came in and smiled
He seemed a little tired
He seemed to be at peace
He waited……
Then he just stood up
And continued on his way.

I think it was an angel
He just came in and rested
For a while

You are my Lord

❧

You are my Lord
You are my God
I am here for you

I walk with you during those painful moments
I feel the pain of your suffering

My ancestors honored you
I honor you too

You are the wonder of the universe
Stay with me
I will always love you
As you have always loved me….
For thousands of years

❧

Praise to you Lord

Praise to you Lord
You give
You love
You forgive
You watch
You know
You understand
Me

Gentle Caring

Gentle, caring, loving
Like the soft morning light
Touching the dewed grass
Ever so soft
Like a whisper
Your hands

Like the Wind

Like the wind
Blowing gently against my face
Quietly whispering
Softly t ouching
My soul listens
You are a friend

Like a Warm Blanket

Like a warm blanket
Soft and fuzzy
Always there to comfort,
Always there to hold,
Always special,
Always near,
Your friendship
For it has rooted deep inside
Has found my soul
And gently whispered
I am a special friend

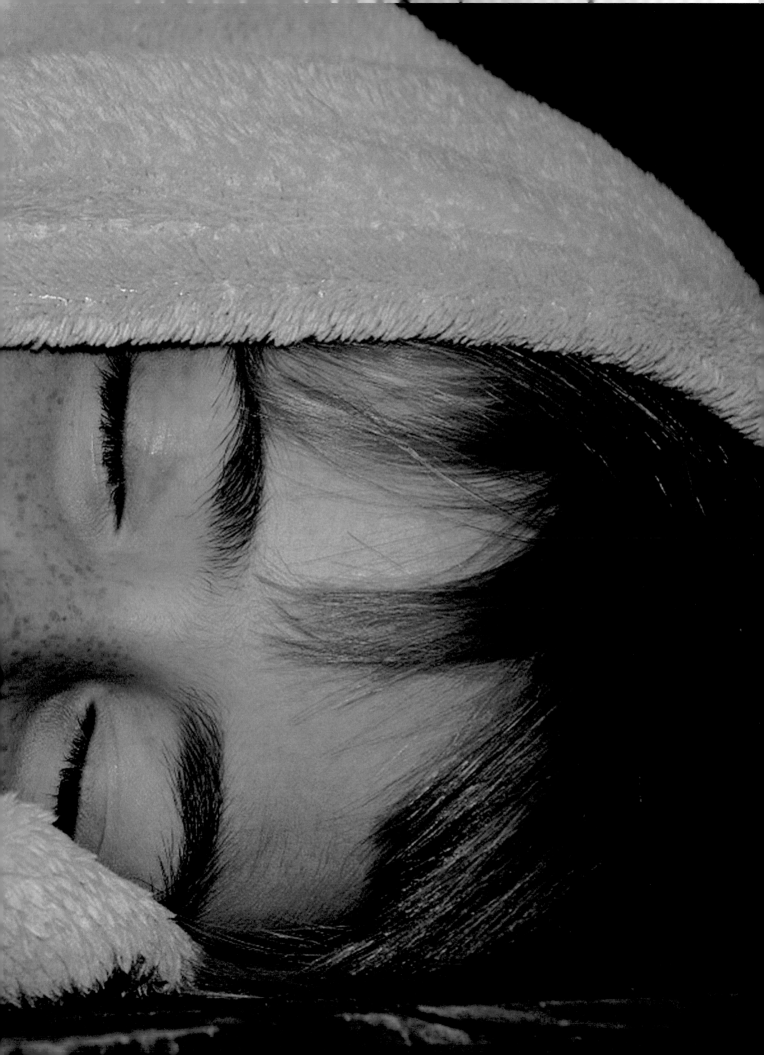

Angel Footprints

Today,
I saw some footprints

They were crossing through my yard

I stood and saw the shape and size

And I quickly knew

An angel had been by.

He left his footprints
On the grass
So I would know that he had passed
On his way to far away
Where all the other angels
wait

Angel Wing

I found an angel wing one day
It was laying on my bed
I picked it up
And knew
That soon she would be back

I placed it on a soft white pillow
And left a little note
It said…..
"I found your wing today,
You must have left it here;
I cannot stay and wait for you
I have a million things to do."

Dear God
You said you would be with me
And carry me through hard times
I swing on a swing from
The tall Oak tree
I close my eyes and swing
Worried, sad, where are you?

I open my eyes
A thousand people are looking up at the tree

I stop to look up
You heard my prayers

You are here
I see you
The old tree is no more
It is now
Your cross
How all powerful you are
Dear God

I am swinging from the right side of your cross
How can that be
When I sat on the swing it was an old Oak tree

I look up
And
There you are
You carry me through this difficult time

❧

Printed in the United States
by Baker & Taylor Publisher Services